Soup Maker
- soup making made easy

by Paul Brodel

Introduction

Welcome to Soup Maker - soup making made easy. What could be more satisfying than a hot steaming bowl of your favourite soup on a cold and frosty day? From a Chefs point of view, they are simple, inexpensive and versatile dishes that can be made from virtually any ingredients.

Soups are so simple to make, as you will see from the recipes in this book. If you want to make them even simpler, you could use one of the various types of soup makers/soup Blenders on the market. These will not only help you to make delicious soups, but can also make smoothies and lemonade etc. My recipes show you how to make soups using the traditional method as well as using a Soup Maker/Soup Blender.

My recipes are adaptable, try to be adventurous and swap or change ingredients for others. As an example, try using a sweet potato instead of an ordinary one, add spices to give your soup that kick. There's no end to what you can do. You are only limited by your imagination.

Have a fabulous time.

Helpful Hints: When using a soup maker/soup blender

Always follow the manufacturer's instructions. This book is to be used as a guide. Always ensure your food is thoroughly cooked prior to consumption. When making soup in the soup maker/soup blender, do not over fill.

Where I have used kidney beans in a recipe, I always use tinned as there is no need to soak. Always ensure all vegetables, pulses etc. have been thoroughly washed.

I like to use chicken or beef stock in my soups, but you can always replace this with vegetable stock if you prefer.

At the end of cooking, I often add a little double cream to my soups to make it slightly smoother, creamier and more luxurious. This is not a necessity and can be left out.

Where the ingredients state mascarpone, you can substitute it for cream cheese. Remember, things like milk and cream are best added at the end of cooking. Fresh herbs add an amazing flavour to soups, but I also use dried as well. Feel free to use what you have available.

There are many different ways to make soups, and in this book I have tried and tested all of the recipes in various ways, using a saucepan and different appliances: a soup maker and a soup blender.
In this book, I give instructions for four different methods of cooking your soups. In a saucepan, for soup makers, and for soup blenders. Please use whatever is applicable to you.

Cooking instructions will be listed for each method in the following order:
a. **Sauce Pan** which you manually blend at the end of cooking.
b. **Soup Maker** which heat only and you blend at the end (if desired). These require you to manually set the time and temperature.
c. **Programmable Soup Blender** which can blend and heat simultaneously, with additional filters for chunky soup. These have pre-set programs for smooth and chunky soups.
d. **Manual Soup Blender** which heat only and you blend at the end (if desired). These have pre-set cooking temperatures, and have a removable blade for easy cleaning.

Use the recipes in this book as a guide and follow the manufacturer's instructions.

Contents / Index
Soup Maker
- soup making made easy

Smooth Soups

Chunky Soups

Stocks

Stocks are a great base for making tasty, wholesome soups. Although I have used stock cubes in my soup recipes, you may prefer to make your own stock. I have given you the recipes of four main flavours of stocks; chicken, beef, lamb and fish. These stock recipes can be varied to your own preference.

Chicken Stock

Chicken bones
 (from a chicken carcass)
1 Celery stalk or 1/4 tsp celery salt
7 Peppercorns
3 Bay leaves
1 tsp Mixed herbs or bouquet garni
1 Onion (cut in half)
2 to 3 litres boiling water
2 Carrots (peeled)
1 Swede (peeled) optional
(add for the last two hours then remove)
1 Leek (trimmed)
Parsley sprigs (or pinch of dried)
Add giblets to make a richer stock

Beef Stock

Beef bones
(browned using a little oil in a frying pan)
1 Onion (peeled and halved)
1 Carrot (peeled and halved)
1 Celery stalk
1 Parsley sprig (or pinch dried)
1 Bay leaf
6 Peppercorns
1 Blade black mace (optional)
1 tsp Mixed dried herbs
  (or bouquet garni)
2 to 3 litres boiling water
Season with salt and pepper

In a pan, bring to the boil and simmer all stock ingredients with the lid on for 6-10 hours, skimming when needed to remove froth and fat.
Sieve and use when cooking soup, casserole, gravy, curry, sauces etc.

Lamb Stock

Lamb bones
(browned using a little oil in a frying pan)
1 Onion (peeled and halved)
1 Carrot (peeled and halved)
1 Celery stalk
1 Parsley sprig (or pinch dried)
1 Bay leaf
6 Peppercorns
1 tsp Mixed dried herbs (or bouquet garni)
2 to 3 litres boiling water
Season with salt and pepper

In a pan, bring to the boil and simmer all stock ingredients with the lid on for 6-10 hours, skimming when needed to remove froth and fat.
Sieve and use when cooking soup, casserole, gravy, curry, sauces etc.

Fish Stock

½ kilo Fish trimmings (heads, tails, fins, etc)
1 Onion (peeled and halved)
1 Celery stalk or ¼ tsp celery salt
Parsley sprigs (or ¼ tsp dried parsley)
2 Bay leaves
7 Peppercorns
½ tsp Mixed herbs or bouquet garni
250ml White wine
¼ tsp Granulated sugar
Pinch of salt and white pepper

In a pan, bring to the boil and simmer all stock ingredients with the lid on for 6-10 hours, skimming when needed to remove excess froth and fat, sieve and use in cooking.

Cooking is an art, not a precise science

Why not be adventurous? There are so many wonderful fresh vegetables, herbs, spices, meats and fish available; try adding or subtracting ingredients to tailor the soups to your preference.

Ideas for swapping ingredients:

Potatoes - Sweet Potatoes
Carrots - Butternut Squash
Parsnips - Turnips
Rocket - Water Cress
Leeks - Onions
Turnips - Radishes
Curly Kale - Savoy Cabbage
Bacon - Ham
Prawns - Scallops
Turkey Mince - Chicken Mince
Chicken Stock - Vegetable Stock
Mascarpone - Cream Cheese
Grated Cheese - Basil Pesto
Chilli Cheese - Red Pepper Pesto
Mustard - Pesto

I have used both fresh and dried herbs in this book, feel free to use either.

When referring to vegetables in this book:

1 Potato = 240g (peeled)
1 Carrot = 105g (peeled)
1 Onion = 120g (peeled)
1 Leek = 120g (peeled & prepared)
1 Parsnip = 115g (peeled and prepared)
1/4 Swede = 240g (peeled & prepared)

Top tips

Try to purchase vegetables which are in season. This will help you fully appreciate their heightened flavour and they are normally better value.

Always look at the prices per kilo as buy-one-get-one-free offers may not always be the best deal.

Always look at the bottom shelves, this is normally where the cheapest and best value ranges are.

Try shopping in local markets and butchers shops where you may find cheaper prices and better quality, longer lasting food.

When buying produce like potatoes, I always try to buy a sack from a local farmer. Keep them in a cool, dark place where they will last longer than washed potatoes. They are normally much better value too.

Certain vegetables work well if you roast them first. This helps to bring out more of their flavour. To do this, coat them in a little oil and place them in a hot oven for 20 minutes to caramelise them. Then follow as per my recipes.

When adding cornflour to a recipe to thicken the soup, ensure the soup is very hot, otherwise you may have to bring the soup back to the boil, in order for the cornflour to work (always mix cornflour with a little cold water first).

If you want your soup to go further why not add some cooked pasta to your finished soup.

Smooth
Soups

Asparagus & Parma Ham

Smooth

Ingredients **Serves 2-4**
7 Asparagus (sliced)
1 Potato (peeled & cubed)
1 Onion (peeled & sliced)
3 Slices Parma ham (chopped)
1 Chicken stock cube
¼ tsp Mixed herbs
50ml Double cream
Pinch salt & pepper
Croutons (optional)

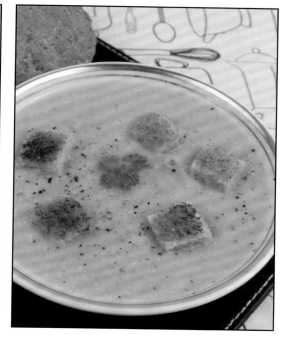

Method

1. Put the asparagus, potato, onion, Parma ham, stock cube and mixed herbs in a pan or the soup maker/soup blender.
2. Fill with water (approx 600ml) or to the soup level and season.

   a. Using pan method, bring to the boil and simmer for 20 minutes.
   b. Using a soup maker, use high heat setting for 7 minutes, then low/simmer settings for 20 minutes.
   c. Using a programmable soup blender, press smooth soup.
   d. Using a manual soup blender, set time for 20 minutes.
   (Whichever is applicable to your appliance).
3. Once finished cooking, stir in cream.
   a. Using pan method, blend at the end of cooking.
   b. Using soup maker method, use the built-in blender.
   c. Using programmable soup blender, should be ready to serve
   d. Using manual soup blender, blend to desired consistency.
4. Garnish with croutons and serve.

Beef Curry

Ingredients **Serves 2-4**

100g Minced beef
50g Rice
1 Carrot (peeled & sliced)
1 tsp Dark soy sauce
1 Onion (peeled & sliced)
13g Butter
¼ tsp Garlic salt
2 Beef stock cubes
2 tbsp Sweet chilli sauce
1 tsp Curry powder
        or curry paste
½ tsp White pepper
Pinch salt

Method

1. Put the minced beef, rice, carrot, dark soy sauce, onion, sweet chilli, butter, garlic salt, curry powder, beef stock cubes into a pan or the soup maker/soup blender.
2. Fill with water (approx 600ml) or to the soup level and season.
   a. Using pan method, bring to the boil and simmer for 20 minutes.
   b. Using a soup maker, use high heat setting for 7 minutes, then low/simmer settings for 20 minutes.
   c. Using a programmable soup blender, press smooth soup.
   d. Using a manual soup blender, set time for 20 minutes) (whichever is applicable to your appliance).
3. Once finished cooking,
   a. Using pan method, blend at the end of cooking.
   b. Using soup maker method, use the built-in blender.
   c. Using programmable soup blender, should be ready to serve
   d. Using manual soup blender, blend to desired consistency.

4. Serve with a crusty bread roll.

Beetroot & Apple

Ingredients **Serves 2-4**
100g Beetroot (cooked & cubed)
½ Carrot (peeled & sliced)
1 Potato (peeled & cubed)
55g Apple (peeled & sliced)
½ Onion (peeled & sliced)
1 Stick celery (sliced)
1 tsp Dijon mustard
13g Butter
1 Chicken stock cube
Pinch salt & pepper
Cheese pastry croutons (see page 27)

Method

1. Put the beetroot, carrot, potato, apple, onion, celery, dijon mustard, butter, stock cube in a pan or the soup maker/soup blender.
2. Fill with water (approx 600ml) or to the soup level and season.

   a. Using pan method, bring to the boil and simmer for 20 minutes.
   b. Using a soup maker, use high heat setting for 7 minutes then low/ simmer settings for 20 minutes.
   c. Using a programmable soup blender, press smooth soup.
   d. Using a manual soup blender, set time for 20 minutes. (Whichever is applicable to your appliance).
3. Once finished cooking,
   a. Using pan method, blend at the end of cooking.
   b. Using soup maker method, use the built-in blender.
   c. Using programmable soup blender, should be ready to serve
   d. Using manual soup blender, blend to desired consistency.
4. Serve with cheese pastry croutons as per recipe on page 27.

15

Butternut Squash & Orange Smooth

Ingredients   Serves 2-4
400g Butternut squash
    (peeled & sliced)
1 Potato (peeled & cubed)
1 Onion (peeled & sliced)
¼ tsp Garlic salt
1 Chicken stock cube
50ml Orange juice
1 tbsp Cranberry sauce
Pinch salt & pepper
Grated nutmeg (optional)

Method

1. Put butternut squash ,potato, onion, garlic salt, stock cube, orange juice, cranberry into a pan or the soup maker/soup blender.
2. Fill with water (approx 600ml) or to the soup level and season.
    a. Using pan method, bring to the boil and simmer for 20 minutes.
    b. Using a soup maker, use high heat setting for 7 minutes, then low/simmer settings for 20 minutes.
    c. Using a programmable soup blender, press smooth soup.
    d. Using a manual soup blender, set time for 20 minutes.
    (Whichever is applicable to your appliance).
3. Once finished cooking,
    a. Using pan method, blend at the end of cooking.
    b. Using soup maker method, use the built-in blender.
    c. Using programmable soup blender, should be ready to serve
    d. Using manual soup blender, blend to desired consistency.
4. Garnish with grated nutmeg and serve.

> For plain butternut squash soup, replace the orange juice with water and leave out the cranberry sauce.

Carrot & Lentil

Smooth

Ingredients **Serves 2-4**
50g Red split lentils
3 Carrots (peeled & sliced)
1 Onion (peeled & sliced)
½ tsp Garlic salt
½ tsp Mixed herbs
1 Chicken stock cube
Pinch salt & pepper
1 tbsp Fresh parsley

Method

1. Put the lentils, carrot, onion, garlic salt, mixed herbs, stock cube in a pan or the soup maker/soup blender.
2. Fill with water (approx 600ml) or to the soup level and season.
   a. Using pan method, bring to the boil and simmer for 20 minutes.
   b. Using a soup maker, use high heat setting for 7 minutes, then low/simmer settings for 20 minutes.
   c. Using a programmable soup blender, press smooth soup.
   d. Using a manual soup blender, set time for 20 minutes.
   (Whichever is applicable to your appliance).
3. Once finished cooking,
   a. Using pan method, blend at the end of cooking.
   b. Using soup maker method, use the built-in blender.
   c. Using programmable soup blender, should be ready to serve
   d. Using manual soup blender, blend to desired consistency.
4. Garnish with parsley and serve.

17

Chicken & Tarragon

Smooth

Ingredients **Serves 2-4**
100g chicken breast
    (small cubed)
1 Onion (peeled & quartered)
160g Celeriac
½ Potato (peeled & cubed)
½ tsp Garlic salt
½ tsp Mixed herbs
1 Chicken stock cube
50ml Double cream
Pinch salt & pepper
5g Fresh tarragon (chopped)

Method

1. Put the chicken, onion, celeriac, potato, garlic salt, mixed herbs, stock cube in a pan or the soup maker/soup blender.
2. Fill with water (approx 600ml) or to the soup level and season.
   a. Using pan method, bring to the boil and simmer for 20 minutes.
   b. Using a soup maker, use high heat setting for 7 minutes, then low/ simmer settings for 20 minutes.
   c. Using a programmable soup blender, press smooth soup.
   d. Using a manual soup blender, set time for 20 minutes. (Whichever is applicable to your appliance).
3. Once finished cooking, stir in cream.
   a. Using pan method, blend at the end of cooking.
   b. Using soup maker method, use the built-in blender.
   c. Using programmable soup blender, should be ready to serve
   d. Using manual soup blender, blend to desired consistency.
4. Garnish with chopped tarragon and serve.

Courgette & Pea

Smooth

Ingredients **Serves 2-4**
150g Courgette (sliced)
1 Onion (peeled & quartered)
½ Potato
   (peeled & quartered)
150g Frozen peas
1 tsp Mint jelly
½ tsp Garlic salt
½ tsp Mixed herbs
1 Chicken stock cube
Pinch salt & pepper
50ml Double cream
1 tbsp Fresh parsley

Method

1. Put the courgette, onion, potato, peas, mint jelly, garlic salt, mixed herbs, stock cube in a pan or the soup maker/soup blender.
2. Fill with water (approx 500ml) or to the soup level and season.

   a. Using pan method, bring to the boil and simmer for 20 minutes.
   b. Using a soup maker, use high heat setting for 7 minutes, then low/simmer settings for 20 minutes.
   c. Using a programmable soup blender, press smooth soup.
   d. Using a manual soup blender, set time for 20 minutes.
   (Whichever is applicable to your appliance).
3. Once finished cooking, stir in cream.
   a. Using pan method, blend at the end of cooking.
   b. Using soup maker method, use the built-in blender.
   c. Using programmable soup blender, should be ready to serve
   d. Using manual soup blender, blend to desired consistency.
4. Garnish with fresh parsley and serve.

19

Cream of Chicken

Ingredients **Serves 2-4**

180g Chicken breast
    (small cubed)
½ Onion (peeled & sliced)
1 Potato (peeled & cubed
50g Celery
½ tsp Garlic salt
½ tsp Dried sage
1 Chicken stock cube
Pinch salt & pepper
2 tbsp Cornflour -
    mixed with a little water
50ml Double cream
5g Chives (chopped)

Method

1. Put the chicken, onion, potato, celery, garlic salt, dried sage, stock cube, in a pan or the soup maker/soup blender.
2. Fill with water (approx 600ml) or to the soup level and season.
   a. Using pan method, bring to the boil and simmer for 20 minutes.
   b. Using a soup maker, use high heat setting for 7 minutes, then low/simmer settings for 20 minutes.
   c. Using a programmable soup blender, press smooth soup.
   d. Using a manual soup blender, set time for 20 minutes.
   (Whichever is applicable to your appliance).

3. Once finished cooking, stir the cornflour into the hot soup and add the cream.
   a. Using pan method, blend at the end of cooking.
   b. Using soup maker method, use the built-in blender.
   c. Using programmable soup blender, should be ready to serve
   d. Using manual soup blender, blend to desired consistency.
4. Garnish with chopped chives and serve.

Creamy Parsnip

Ingredients **Serves 2-4**
2 Parsnips (peeled & sliced)
1 Potato (peeled & cubed)
1 Onion (peeled & sliced)
½ tbs Sesame seed oil
1 tsp Honey
1 Chicken stock cube
Pinch salt & pepper
50ml Double cream
1 tbsp Toasted sesame seeds
(Toast raw sesame seeds in a hot pan)

Method

1. Put the parsnip, potato, onion, stock cube, sesame oil and honey in a pan or the soup maker/soup blender.
2. Fill with water (approx 600ml) or to the soup level and season.
   a. Using pan method, bring to the boil and simmer for 20 minutes.
   b. Using a soup maker, use high heat setting for 7 minutes, then low/simmer settings for 20 minutes.
   c. Using a programmable soup blender, press smooth soup.
   d. Using a manual soup blender, set time for 20 minutes.
   (Whichever is applicable to your appliance).

3. Once finished cooking, stir in the cream.
   a. Using pan method, blend at the end of cooking.
   b. Using soup maker method, use the built-in blender.
   c. Using programmable soup blender, should be ready to serve
   d. Using manual soup blender, blend to desired consistency.
4. Garnish with toasted sesame seeds and serve.

21

Creamy Vegetable

Ingredients **Serves 2-4**

1 Carrot (peeled & sliced)
1 Potato (peeled & cubed)
1 Onion (peeled & sliced)
¼ Swede (peeled & cubed)
1 Chicken stock cube
Pinch salt & pepper
50ml Double cream
25g Parmesan or alternative
    hard cheese

Method

1. Put the carrot, potato, swede onion, stock cube in a pan or the soup maker/soup blender.
2. Fill with water (approx 600ml) or to the soup level and season.

   a. Using pan method, bring to the boil and simmer for 20 minutes.
   b. Using a soup maker, use high heat setting for 7 minutes, then low/ simmer settings for 20 minutes.
   c. Using a programmable soup blender, press smooth soup.
   d. Using a manual soup blender, set time for 20 minutes. (Whichever is applicable to your appliance).
3. Once finished cooking, stir in the cream.
   a. Using pan method, blend at the end of cooking.
   b. Using soup maker method, use the built-in blender.
   c. Using programmable soup blender, should be ready to serve
   d. Using manual soup blender, blend to desired consistency.
4. Garnish with Parmesan shavings and serve.

Instead of cheese try adding a spoonful of pesto.

Fennel & Cumin

Smooth

Ingredients **Serves 2-4**

1 Fennel (sliced)
1 Potato (peeled & cubed)
1 Onion (peeled & sliced)
13g Butter
¼ tsp Cumin powder
1 Chicken stock cube
50ml Double cream
Pinch salt & pepper
¼ tsp White pepper
¼ tsp Mixed dried herbs

Method

1. Put the fennel, potato, onion, butter, stock cube,mixed dried herbs and cumin powder in a pan or the soup maker/soup blender.
2. Fill with water (approx 600ml) or to the soup level and season.

   a. Using pan method, bring to the boil and simmer for 20 minutes.
   b. Using a soup maker, use high heat setting for 7 minutes, then low/simmer settings for 20 minutes.
   c. Using a programmable soup blender, press smooth soup.
   d. Using a manual soup blender, set time for 20 minutes.
   (Whichever is applicable to your appliance).
3. Once finished cooking, stir in the cream.
   a. Using pan method, blend at the end of cooking.
   b. Using soup maker method, use the built-in blender.
   c. Using programmable soup blender, should be ready to serve
   d. Using manual soup blender, blend to desired consistency.
4. Serve with a crusty bread roll.

Green Lentil & Courgette

Ingredients **Serves 2-4**
1 Carrot (peeled & sliced)
1 Parsnip (peeled & cubed)
1 Leek (peeled & sliced)
1 Courgette (sliced)
1 Slice of Streaky Bacon
50g Green Lentils
1 Chicken stock cube
Pinch salt & pepper
Freshly ground pepper
(optional)

Method

1. Put the leek, carrot, parsnip, courgette, bacon, stock cube, and lentils into a pan or the soup maker/soup blender.
2. Fill with water (approx 600ml) or to the soup level and season.
   a. Using pan method, bring to the boil and simmer for 20 minutes.
   b. Using a soup maker, use high heat setting for 7 minutes, then low/simmer settings for 20 minutes.

   c. Using a programmable soup blender, press smooth soup.
   d. Using a manual soup blender, set time for 20 minutes. (Whichever is applicable to your appliance).
3. Once finished cooking,
   a. Using pan method, blend at the end of cooking.
   b. Using soup maker method, use the built-in blender.
   c. Using programmable soup blender, should be ready to serve
   d. Using manual soup blender, blend to desired consistency.
4. Garnish with freshly ground pepper and serve.

Instead of green lentils try red split lentils.

Italian Bean

Ingredients **Serves 2-4**

200g Tinned chopped tomatoes
200g Tinned mixed beans in
    spicy sauce
2 Fresh tomatoes (quartered)
½ Red onion (peeled & sliced)
½ tbsp Balsamic glaze
½ tsp Garlic salt
½ tsp Mixed herbs
1 Chicken stock cube
Pinch salt & pepper
10 Fresh basil leaves
12 Mozzarella balls (optional)
Feta Crouton (optional see page 56)

Method

1. Put the chopped tomatoes, mixed beans, fresh tomatoes, red onion, balsamic, garlic salt, mixed herbs stock cube in a pan or the soup maker/soup blender.

2. Fill with water (approx 300ml) or to the soup level and season.
   a. Using pan method, bring to the boil and simmer for 20 minutes.
   b. Using a soup maker, use high heat setting for 7 minutes, then low/ simmer settings for 20 minutes.
   c. Using a programmable soup blender, press smooth soup.
   d. Using a manual soup blender, set time for 20 minutes. (Whichever is applicable to your appliance).
3. Once finished cooking,
   a. Using pan method, blend at the end of cooking.
   b. Using soup maker method, use the built-in blender.
   c. Using programmable soup blender, should be ready to serve
   d. Using manual soup blender, blend to desired consistency.
4. Garnish with basil leaves, mozzarella balls or feta croutons, (refer to page 56) and serve.

25

Leek and Potato

Smooth

Ingredients   **Serves 2-4**

1 Leek (sliced)
1 Potato (peeled & cubed)
½ tsp Garlic salt
½ tsp Mixed herbs
1 Chicken stock cube
100ml Double cream
Pinch salt & pepper
100g Ready rolled puff pastry
45g Gruyere cheese (grated)

Method

1. Put the leek, potato, garlic salt, mixed herbs, stock cube in a pan or the soup maker/soup blender.
2. Fill with water (approx 600ml) or to the soup level and season.
   a. Using pan method, bring to the boil and simmer for 20 minutes.
   b. Using a soup maker, use high heat setting for 7 minutes, then low/ simmer settings for 20 minutes.
   c. Using a programmable soup blender, press smooth soup.
   d. Using a manual soup blender, set time for 20 minutes.
   (Whichever is applicable to your appliance).
3. Once finished cooking, stir in the cream.
   a. Using pan method, blend at the end of cooking.
   b. Using soup maker method, use the built-in blender.
   c. Using programmable soup blender, should be ready to serve
   d. Using manual soup blender, blend to desired consistency.
4. Cut the puff pastry into 3cm squares, sprinkle with cheese and place on a baking tray. Cook in a pre heated oven 180°c (gas mark 4 / 350°f) for 12 minutes or until golden brown.
5. Serve the soup with the puff pastry on top.

For extra flavour, add a teaspoon of your favourite mustard

27

Moroccan Lamb

Ingredients **Serves 2-4**

100g Lamb mince
200g Tinned Chickpeas (drained)
1 Carrot (peeled & sliced)
1 Onion (peeled & sliced)
½ Sweet potato (peeled & diced)
1 Garlic clove (peeled & chopped)
200g Tinned Chopped tomatoes
50g Dried apricots
1 tsp Honey
¼ tsp Paprika
¼ tsp Cinnamon
¼ tsp Tumeric
1 Chicken stock cube
Pinch salt & pepper
Coriander to garnish

Method

1. Put the lamb mince, chickpeas, carrot, onion, sweet potato, garlic, tined tomatoes, dried apricots, honey, paprika, cinnamon, tumeric and stock cube in a pan or the soup maker/soup blender.
2. Fill with water (approx 600ml) or to the soup level and season.
   a. Using pan method, bring to the boil and simmer for 20 minutes.
   b. Using a soup maker, use high heat setting for 7 minutes, then low/simmer settings for 20 minutes.
   c. Using a programmable soup blender, press smooth soup.
   d. Using a manual soup blender, set time for 20 minutes.
      (Whichever is applicable to your appliance).
3. Once finished cooking,
   a. Using pan method, blend at the end of cooking.
   b. Using soup maker method, use the built-in blender.
   c. Using programmable soup blender, should be ready to serve
   d. Using manual soup blender, blend to desired consistency.
4. Garnish with coriander and serve with a crusty bread roll.

This can be made as a chunky soup by chopping the ingredients finely (following relevant method).

Mushroom & Sherry

Smooth

Ingredients **Serves 2-4**

200g Button mushrooms
 (washed & halved)
1 Onion (chopped)
2 tbsp Sweet sherry (optional)
15g Butter
2 tbsp Cornflour -
 mixed with a little water
100ml Double cream
½ tsp Garlic salt
1 Chicken stock cube
Pinch salt & pepper

Method

1. Add the mushroom, onion, butter, sweet sherry, garlic salt and the stock cube in a pan or the soup maker/soup blender.
2. Fill with water (approx 600ml) or to the soup level and season.

   a. Using pan method, bring to the boil and simmer for 20 minutes.
   b. Using a soup maker, use high heat setting for 7 minutes, then low/simmer settings for 20 minutes.
   c. Using a programmable soup blender, press smooth soup.
   d. Using a manual soup blender, set time for 20 minutes.
      (Whichever is applicable to your appliance).
3. Once finished cooking, stir in cornflour into the hot soup and then add the cream.
   a. Using pan method, blend at the end of cooking.
   b. Using soup maker method, use the built-in blender.
   c. Using programmable soup blender, should be ready to serve.
   d. Using manual soup blender, blend to desired consistency.

4. Serve with a crusty bread roll.

Rocket & Herb Cheese
Smooth

Ingredients **Serves 2-4**
70g Fresh rocket
1 Potato (peeled & cubed)
1 Onion (peeled & sliced)
75g Garlic & herb cream
cheese
1 Chicken stock cube
Pinch salt & pepper
1 tbsp Toasted sesame seeds

Method

1. Put the rocket, potato, onion, stock cube in a pan or the soup maker/soup blender.
2. Fill with water (approx 600ml) or to the soup level and season.
   a. Using pan method, bring to the boil and simmer for 20 minutes.
   b. Using a soup maker, use high heat setting for 7 minutes, then low/simmer settings for 20 minutes.
   c. Using a programmable soup blender, press smooth soup.
   d. Using a manual soup blender, set time for 20 minutes.
      (Whichever is applicable to your appliance).
3. Once finished cooking, stir in cream cheese.
   a. Using pan method, blend at the end of cooking.
   b. Using soup maker method, use the built-in blender.
   c. Using programmable soup blender, should be ready to serve.
   d. Using manual soup blender, blend to desired consistency.
4. Garnish with a sprinkle of toasted sesame seeds and serve.

31

Root Vegetable

Ingredients **Serves 2-4**

1 Carrot (peeled & sliced)
1 Sweet potato (peeled & cubed)
1 Parsnip (peeled & sliced)
1 Onion (peeled & sliced)
¼ tsp Garlic salt
50ml Double cream
1 Chicken stock cube
½ tsp Mixed herbs
Pinch salt & pepper

Method

1. Put carrot, sweet potato, parsnip, onion, stock cube, garlic salt and mixed herbs in a pan or the soup maker/soup blender.
2. Fill with water (approx 600ml) or to the soup level and season.
   a. Using pan method, bring to the boil and simmer for 20 minutes.
   b. Using a soup maker, use high heat setting for 7 minutes, then low/ simmer settings for 20 minutes.
   c. Using a programmable soup blender, press smooth soup.
   d. Using a manual soup blender, set time for 20 minutes.
      (Whichever is applicable to your appliance).
3. Once finished cooking, stir in the cream.
   a. Using pan method, blend at the end of cooking.
   b. Using soup maker method, use the built-in blender.
   c. Using programmable soup blender, should be ready to serve.
   d. Using manual soup blender, blend to desired consistency.
   4. Serve

For extra flavour add a teaspoon of mustard

Smoked Bacon & Lentil

Ingredients **Serves 2-4**

1 Carrot (peeled & sliced)
1 Potato (peeled & cubed)
1 Onion (peeled & sliced)
50g Streaky smoked bacon
　　(sliced)
40g Split green lentils
1 Chicken stock cube
50ml Double cream
Pinch salt & pepper
24 croutons

Method

1. Put the carrot, potato, onion, streaky smoked bacon, lentils and stock cube in a pan or the soup maker/soup blender.
2. Fill with water (approx 600ml) or to the soup level and season.
   a. Using pan method, bring to the boil and simmer for 20 minutes.
   b. Using a soup maker, use high heat setting for 7 minutes, then low/ simmer settings for 20 minutes.
   c. Using a programmable soup blender, press smooth soup.
   d. Using a manual soup blender, set time for 20 minutes. (Whichever is applicable to your appliance).
3. Once finished cooking, stir in the cream.
   a. Using pan method, blend at the end of cooking.
   b. Using soup maker method, use the built-in blender.
   c. Using programmable soup blender, should be ready to serve
   d. Using manual soup blender, blend to desired consistency.
4. Garnish with croutons and serve.

Instead of green lentils try red split lentils.

Spicy Cauliflower

Ingredients **Serves 2-4**

½ Cauliflower (cut into florets)
1 Potato (peeled & cubed)
1 Onion (peeled & sliced)
½ tsp Cumin
1 Chicken stock cube
1 tbsp Mascarpone
¼ tsp White pepper
Pinch salt
50g Cheddar cheese (grated)

Method

1. Put the cauliflower, potato,onion, cumin, white pepper, stock cube in a pan or the soup maker/soup blender.
2. Fill with water (approx 600ml) or to the soup level and season.
   a. Using pan method, bring to the boil and simmer for 20 minutes.
   b. Using a soup maker, use high heat setting for 7 minutes, then low/simmer settings for 20 minutes.

   c. Using a programmable soup blender, press smooth soup.
   d. Using a manual soup blender, set time for 20 minutes. (Whichever is applicable to your appliance).
3. Once finished cooking, stir in the mascarpone.
   a. Using pan method, blend at the end of cooking.
   b. Using soup maker method, use the built-in blender.
   c. Using programmable soup blender, should be ready to serve
   d. Using manual soup blender, blend to desired consistency.
4. Garnish with grated cheddar cheese and serve.

For a plain cauliflower soup, leave out the cumin and change mascarpone for 50ml of double cream.

Stilton & Walnut

Smooth

Ingredients **Serves 2-4**
1 Carrot (peeled & sliced)
1 Potato (peeled & cubed)
1 Onion (peeled & sliced)
100g Watercress
50g Stilton cheese (crumbled)
1 Chicken stock cube
50ml Double cream
Pinch salt & pepper
25g Walnuts (chopped)

Method

1. Put the carrot, potato,and onion, stock cube, Stilton and watercress in a pan or the soup maker/soup blender.
2. Fill with water (approx 600ml) or to the soup level and season.
   a. Using pan method, bring to the boil and simmer for 20 minutes.
   b. Using a soup maker, use high heat setting for 7 minutes, then low/simmer settings for 20 minutes.
   c. Using a programmable soup blender, press smooth soup.
   d. Using a manual soup blender, set time for 20 minutes. (Whichever is applicable to your appliance).
3. Once finished cooking, stir in the cream.
   a. Using pan method, blend at the end of cooking.
   b. Using soup maker method, use the built-in blender.
   c. Using programmable soup blender, should be ready to serve
   d. Using manual soup blender, blend to desired consistency.
4. Garnish with chopped walnut pieces and serve.

36

Tomato

Smooth

Ingredients **Serves 2-4**
1 Onion (peeled & sliced)
400g tinned chopped tomatoes
1 Beef tomato (cut into 8)
1 tbsp Tomato puree
1 Chicken stock cube
¼ tsp Dried mixed herbs
Pinch salt & pepper
10 Fresh basil leaves

Method

1. Put the onion, chopped tomatoes, beef tomato, tomato puree, stock cube, and mixed herbs in a pan or the soup maker/soup blender.
2. Fill with water (approx 600ml) or to the soup level and season.
   a. Using pan method, bring to the boil and simmer for 20 minutes.
   b. Using a soup maker, use high heat setting for 7 minutes, then low/simmer settings for 20 minutes.

   c. Using a programmable soup blender, press smooth soup.
   d. Using a manual soup blender, set time for 20 minutes.
      (Whichever is applicable to your appliance).
3. Once finished cooking,
   a. Using pan method, blend at the end of cooking.
   b. Using soup maker method, use the built-in blender.
   c. Using programmable soup blender, should be ready to serve
   d. Using manual soup blender, blend to desired consistency.
4. Garnish with fresh basil leaves and serve.

Vegetable & Cheese

Smooth

Ingredients **Serves 2-4**

1 Onion (quartered)
1 Potato (peeled & cubed)
1 Parsnip (peeled & cubed)
85g Cauliflower
     (cut into florets)
1 tsp English mustard
¼ tsp White pepper
¼ tsp Garlic salt
½ tsp Mixed herbs
1 Chicken stock cube
100g Strong cheddar cheese
Pinch salt & pepper
1 tbsp Fresh chopped parsley

Method

1. Put the onion, potato, parsnip, cauliflower, mustard, white pepper, garlic salt, mixed herbs, white pepper, stock cube in a pan or the soup maker/soup blender.
2. Fill with water (approx 600ml) or to the soup level and season.
   a. Using pan method, bring to the boil and simmer for 20 minutes.
   b. Using a soup maker, use high heat setting for 7 minutes, then low/ simmer settings for 20 minutes.
   c. Using a programmable soup blender, press smooth soup.
   d. Using a manual soup blender, set time for 20 minutes. (Whichever is applicable to your appliance).
3. Once finished cooking,
   a. Using pan method, blend at the end of cooking.
   b. Using soup maker method, use the built-in blender.
   c. Using programmable soup blender, should be ready to serve
   d. Using manual soup blender, blend to desired consistency.
4. Garnish with grated cheese, chopped parsley and serve.

You can use butternut squash or sweet potato instead of cauliflower.

Chunky Soups

Chicken & Smoked Paprika Chunky

Ingredients **Serves 2-4**

145g Chicken breast (cubed)
200g Tinned chopped tomatoes
½ Sweet potato
  (peeled & cubed)
½ Onion (peeled & sliced)
½ tsp Smoked paprika
½ Red pepper sliced
1 Chicken stock cube
¼ tsp Dried mixed herbs
Pinch salt & pepper
50g Chorizo (finely chopped)

Method

1. Put the chicken breast, chopped tomatoes, sweet potato, onion, smoked paprika, red pepper, stock cube, mixed herbs and chorizo in a pan or the soup maker/soup blender. If you're using a soup blender with the filter for chunky soups, place the ingredients around the outside of the filter.

2. Fill with water (approx 600ml) or to the soup level and season.

   a. Using pan method, bring to the boil and simmer for 25 minutes.

   b. Using a soup maker, use high heat setting for 7 minutes, then low/ simmer settings for 25 minutes.

   c. Using a programmable soup blender, press chunky soup.

   d. Using a manual soup blender, set cooking time for 20 minutes, then if desired blend to the consistency you require.
      (Whichever is applicable to your appliance).

3. Serve.

Chinese Pork & Ginger

Chunky

Ingredients **Serves 2-4**

100g Pork mince
1 Carrot (peeled & sliced)
1 Spring onions (sliced)
5g Fresh ginger
   (peeled & finely shredded)
6 Mange tout (sliced)
2 tbsp Sweet chilli sauce
1 tsp Sesame seed oil
1 tsp Dark soy sauce
¼ tsp Garlic salt
1 tbsp Plain flour
1 Chicken stock cube
Pinch salt & pepper
60g Egg noodles

Method

1. Mix together the pork mince and flour. Form into marble size balls.

2. Place the carrots, spring onions, ginger, mange tout, sesame seed oil, dark soy sauce, sweet chilli sauce, garlic salt, egg noodles, stock cube and pork balls in a pan or the soup maker/soup blender. If you're using a soup blender with the filter for chunky soups, place the ingredients around the outside of the filter.

3. Fill with water (approx 600ml) or to the soup level and season.
   a. Using pan method, bring to the boil and simmer for 25 minutes.
   b. Using a soup maker, use high heat setting for 7 minutes, then low/simmer settings for 25 minutes.
   c. Using a programmable soup blender, press chunky soup.
   d. Using a manual soup blender, set cooking time for 20 minutes, then if desired blend to the consistency you require.
   (Whichever is applicable to your appliance).

4. Serve

42

Cock-a-Leekie

Ingredients **Serves 2-4**

100g Chicken breast
    (small cubed)
1 Potato (peeled & cubed)
1 Stick celery (sliced)
½ Leek (finely & sliced)
4 Dried prunes (chopped)
½ tsp Garlic salt
½ tsp Mixed herbs
1 Chicken stock cube
Pinch salt & pepper
1 tbsp Fresh chopped parsley

Method

1. Put the chicken, potato, celery, leek, prunes, garlic salt, stock cube and mixed herbs in a pan or the soup maker/soup blender. If you're using a soup blender with the filter for chunky soups, place the ingredients around the outside of the filter.

2. Fill with water (approx 600ml) or to the soup level and season.
   a. Using pan method, bring to the boil and simmer for 25 minutes.
   b. Using a soup maker, use high heat setting for 7 minutes, then low/ simmer settings for 25 minutes.
   c. Using a programmable soup blender, press chunky soup.
   d. Using a manual soup blender, set cooking time for 20 minutes, then if desired blend to the consistency you require.
   (Whichever is applicable to your appliance).
3. Garnish with fresh parsley and serve.

Curly Kale & Chicken

Chunky

Ingredients   **Serves 2-4**

25g Pearl barley (pre-soaked)
100g Chicken Breast (cubed)
½ Potato (peeled & cubed)
½ Onion (finely chopped)
75g Green curly kale(torn)
    or savoy cabbage (torn)
5g Fresh ginger (peeled & sliced)
1 Carrot (peeled & sliced)
¼ tsp Garlic salt
¼ tsp Mixed herbs
1 Chicken stock cube
Pinch salt & pepper

Method

1. Cover the pearl barley with water and soak for 6 hours or overnight.
2. Put the pearl barley, chicken, potato, onion, Kale, ginger, carrot, garlic salt, mixed herbs and stock cube into a pan or the soup maker/ soup blender. If you're using a soup blender with the filter for chunky soups, place the ingredients around the outside of the filter.
3. Fill with water (approx 600ml) or to the soup level and season.
   a. Using pan method, bring to the boil and simmer for 45 minutes.
   b. Using a soup maker, use high heat setting for 7 minutes, then low/ simmer settings for 25 minutes.
   c. Using a programmable soup blender, press chunky soup.
   d. Using a manual soup blender, set cooking time for 40 minutes, then if desired blend to the consistency you require.
   (Whichever is applicable to your appliance).
4. Serve.

You can use lamb mince or beef mince instead of chicken.

45

French Onion with Cheese Chunky

Ingredients **Serves 2-4**

3 Onion (peeled & sliced)
1 tbsp Dark soy sauce
1 tsp Dijon mustard
1 tbsp Sesame seed oil
1 tsp Muscovado sugar or
    (1 tsp gravy browning
    & 1 tsp sugar)
½ tsp Garlic salt
½ tsp Mixed herbs
2 Beef stock cubes
Pinch salt & pepper
85g Gruyere cheese
100g Ready rolled puff pastry

Method

1. Put the onion, soy sauce, mustard, sesame oil, sugar, garlic salt, stock cube and mixed herbs into a pan or the soup maker/soup blender. If you're using a soup blender with the filter for chunky soups, place the ingredients around the outside of the filter.
2. Fill with water (approx 700ml) or to the soup level and season.
   a. Using pan method, bring to the boil and simmer for 25 minutes.
   b. Using a soup maker, use high heat setting for 7 minutes, then low/simmer settings for 25 minutes.
   c. Using a programmable soup blender, press chunky soup.
   d. Using a manual soup blender, set cooking time for 20 minutes, then if desired blend to the consistency you require
   (Whichever is applicable to your appliance).
3. Cut the pastry into 3cm squares, place on a baking tray. Cook in a pre heated oven 180°c (gas mark 4 / 350°f).
4. Serve with gruyere cheese and puff pastry top.

This soup can also be served in Yorkshire puddings. French onion soup makes a great base for onion gravy, thicken and pour over sausages.

Green Lentil & French Bean Chunky

Ingredients **Serves 2-4**

50g Green Lentils
100g French beans (sliced)
1 Garlic clove
  (peeled & chopped)
1 tbsp Olive oil
¼ tsp Mixed herbs
1 Chicken stock cube
Pinch salt & pepper
75g Bacon lardons (optional)

Method

1. Put the lentils, french beans, garlic, oil, stock cube, mixed herbs and bacon in a pan or the soup maker/soup blender. If you're using a soup blender with the filter for chunky soups, place the ingredients around the outside of the filter.

2. Fill with water (approx 600ml) or to the soup level and season.
   a. Using pan method, bring to the boil and simmer for 25 minutes.
   b. Using a soup maker, use high heat setting for 7 minutes, then low/ simmer settings for 25 minutes.
   c. Using a programmable soup blender, press chunky soup.
   d. Using a manual soup blender, set cooking time for 20 minutes, then if desired blend to the consistency you require
   (Whichever is applicable to your appliance).
3. Serve.

Ham & Butterbean

Chunky

Ingredients **Serves 2-4**

1 Carrot (peeled & sliced)
1 Potato (peeled & cubed)
1 Onion (peeled & sliced)
110g Butterbeans
(tinned & drained)
50g Ham (chopped)
¼ tsp Garlic salt
1 Chicken stock cube
¼ tsp Mixed herbs
Pinch salt & pepper

Method

1. Put the carrot, potato, onion, butterbeans, ham, garlic salt, mixed herbs and stock cube in a pan or the soup maker/soup blender. If you're using a soup blender with the filter for chunky soups, place the ingredients around the outside of the filter.

2. Fill with water (approx 600ml) or to the soup level and season.
   a. Using pan method, bring to the boil and simmer for 25 minutes.
   b. Using a soup maker, use high heat setting for 7 minutes, then low/simmer settings for 25 minutes.
   c. Using a programmable soup blender, press chunky soup.
   d. Using a manual soup blender, set cooking time for 20 minutes, then if desired blend to the consistency you require
      (Whichever is applicable to your appliance).
3. Serve.

Herb Dumplings with Chicken ^{Chunky}

Ingredients **Serves 2-4**

100g Chicken breast (sliced)
1 Carrot (peeled & sliced)
½ Potato (peeled & cubed)
½ Onion (peeled & sliced)
¼ tsp Garlic salt
1 Chicken stock cube
50g Frozen Peas
Pinch salt & pepper
20g Streaky bacon sliced
1 tbsp Suet
2 tbsp Self raising flour
1 tsp Mixed herbs

Method

1. In a bowl, mix together the flour, suet and half the mixed herbs with a little water to form a dough.
2. Roll the dough into marble sized dumpling balls.
3. Put the chicken, carrot, potato, onion, garlic salt, stock cube, peas, the remaining mixed herbs, streaky bacon and dumplings in a pan or the soup maker/soup blender. If you're using a soup blender with the filter for chunky soups, put the ingredients around the outside of the filter.
4. Fill with water (approx 500ml) or to the soup level and season.
   a. Using pan method, bring to the boil and simmer for 25 minutes.
   b. Using a soup maker, use high heat setting for 7 minutes, then low/simmer settings for 25 minutes.
   c. Using a programmable soup blender, press chunky soup.
   d. Using a manual soup blender, set cooking time for 20 minutes, then if desired blend to the consistency you require
   (Whichever is applicable to your appliance).

...you can change the chicken stock and chicken for minced beef and beef stock.

Hotdog & Sweetcorn

Chunky

Ingredients **Serves 2-4**

1 Potato
  (peeled & finely cubed)
1 Onion
  (peeled & finely chopped)
10g Gherkins (sliced)
140g Hot dogs (sliced)
135g Sweetcorn
1 tsp English mustard
½ tsp Garlic salt
½ tsp Mixed herbs
1 Chicken stock cube
Pinch salt & pepper
1 tbsp Fresh chopped parsley

Method

1. Put the potato, onion, gherkin, hotdogs, sweetcorn, mustard, garlic salt, stock cube and mixed herbs in a pan or the soup maker/ soup blender. If you're using a soup blender with the filter for chunky soups, place the ingredients around the outside of the filter.

2. Fill with water (approx 600ml) or to the soup level and season.
   a. Using pan method, bring to the boil and simmer for 25 minutes.
   b. Using a soup maker, use high heat setting for 7 minutes, then low/ simmer settings for 25 minutes.
   c. Using a programmable soup blender, press chunky soup.
   d. Using a manual soup blender, set cooking time for 20 minutes, then if desired blend to the consistency you require
   (Whichever is applicable to your appliance).
3. Garnish with fresh parsley and serve.

52

Potato, Bean & Chorizo

Chunky

Ingredients **Serves 2-4**

1 Carrot (peeled & diced)
1 Potato (peeled & cubed)
1 Onion (peeled & sliced)
50g Chorizo (sliced)
400g Tinned kidney beans in
        chilli sauce
1 Chicken stock cube
Pinch salt & pepper
2 tbsp Coriander
        (roughly chopped)

Method

1. Put the carrot, potato, onion chorizo and stock cube in a pan or the soup maker/soup blender. If you're using a soup blender with the filter for chunky soups, put the ingredients around the outside of the filter.

2. Fill with water (approx 600ml) or to the soup level and season.
   a. Using pan method, bring to the boil and simmer for 25 minutes.
   b. Using a soup maker, use high heat setting for 7 minutes, then low/ simmer settings for 25 minutes.
   c. Using a programmable soup blender, press chunky soup.
   d. Using a manual soup blender, set cooking time for 20 minutes, then if desired blend to the consistency you require.
   (Whichever is applicable to your appliance).
3. Heat the kidney beans in chilli sauce and stir into the cooked soup.
4. Garnish with coriander and serve.

53

Prawn Thai

Chunky

Ingredients **Serves 2-4**

100g Fresh prawns
   (peeled & tailed)
1 Carrot (peeled & sliced)
1 Spring onion (sliced)
½ Aubergine (cubed)
¼ tsp Garlic salt
5g Fresh ginger (peeled &
finely sliced)
1 tsp Red thai curry paste
1 tbsp Sweet chilli sauce
1 tsp Lime juice
1 Chicken stock cube
50ml Coconut cream
Pinch salt & pepper
50g Spinach leaves
1 tbsp Fresh coriander

Method

1. Put the prawns, carrot, spring onion, aubergine, garlic salt, curry paste, sweet chilli, lime juice, stock cube in a pan or the soup maker/ soup blender. If you're using a soup blender with the filter for chunky soups, place the ingredients around the outside.
2. Fill with water (approx 600ml) or to the soup level and season.
   a. Using pan method, bring to the boil and simmer for 25 minutes.
   b. Using a soup maker, use high heat setting for 7 minutes, then low/ simmer settings for 25 minutes.
   c. Using a programmable soup blender, press chunky soup.
   d. Using a manual soup blender, set cooking time for 20 minutes, then if desired blend to the consistency you require
      (Whichever is applicable to your appliance).
3. Mix in the coconut cream and spinach leaves.
4. Serve with fresh coriander.

You can use chicken instead of prawns, try adding half a teaspoon of fresh chopped lemon grass.

55

Red Onion & Feta Croutons <small>Chunky</small>

Ingredients **Serves 2-4**
3 Red onion (peeled & sliced)
1 tbsp Dark soy sauce
1 tbsp Sesame seed oil
½ tsp Garlic salt
½ tsp Mixed herbs
2 Beef stock cubes
Pinch salt & pepper
Feta croutons
1 tbsp Mayonnaise
4 slices French stick
50g Feta cheese (crumbled)

Method

1. Put the red onion, soy sauce, sesame oil, garlic salt, stock cube and mixed herbs in a pan or the soup maker/soup blender. If you're using a soup blender with the filter for chunky soups, place the ingredients around the outside of the filter.

2. Fill with water (approx 700ml) or to the soup level and season.

  a. Using pan method, bring to the boil and simmer for 25 minutes.
  b. Using a soup maker, use high heat setting for 7 minutes, then low/ simmer settings for 25 minutes.
  c. Using a programmable soup blender, press chunky soup.
  d. Using a manual soup blender, set cooking time for 20 minutes, then if desired blend to the consistency you require
  (Whichever is applicable to your appliance).

3. To make feta croutons spread some mayonnaise over a sliced french stick, cover with feta cheese and grill until brown.

Add 1 tsp Muscovado sugar for a sweeter taste.

Satay Chicken Noodle

Chunky

Ingredients **Serves 2-4**

100g Chicken breast (sliced)
1 Carrot (peeled & sliced)
1 Spring onion (sliced)
5g Fresh ginger
   (peeled & sliced)
25g Egg noodles
1 tbsp Sweet chilli sauce
50g Sweetcorn
2 tsp Peanut butter
2 tsp Sesame seed oil
2 tsp Soy sauce
¼ tsp Garlic salt
1 Chicken stock cube
1 Clove garlic (chopped)
Pinch salt & pepper

Method

1. Put the chicken, carrot, spring onion, ginger, egg noodles, sweet chilli, sweetcorn, peanut butter, sesame oil, soy sauce, garlic salt, garlic and stock cube in a pan or the soup maker/soup blender. If you're using a soup blender with the filter for chunky soups, put the ingredients around the outside.

2. Fill with water (approx 600ml) or to the soup level and season.

   a. Using pan method, bring to the boil and simmer for 25 minutes.

   b. Using a soup maker, use high heat setting for 7 minutes, then low/ simmer settings for 25 minutes.

   c. Using a programmable soup blender, press chunky soup.

   d. Using a manual soup blender, set cooking time for 20 minutes, then if desired blend to the consistency you require (Whichever is applicable to your appliance).

3. Serve.

Scallops & Bacon

Ingredients **Serves 2-4**

200g Queen Scallops
     without roe
1 Onion (finely chopped)
1 Potato (peeled & finely cubed)
135g Sweetcorn
2 Rashers streaky bacon
    (sliced & chopped)
½ tsp Mustard
½ tsp Mixed herbs
1 Chicken stock cube
½ tsp Garlic salt (optional)
Pinch salt & pepper
50ml Double cream

Method

1. Put the scallops, onion, potato, sweetcorn, bacon, mustard, garlic salt, stock cube and mixed herbs into a pan or the soup maker/soup blender. If you're using a soup blender with the filter for chunky soups, place the ingredients around the outside of the filter.

2. Fill with water (approx 600ml) or to the soup level and season.
   a. Using pan method, bring to the boil and simmer for 25 minutes.
   b. Using a soup maker, use high heat setting for 7 minutes, then low/ simmer settings for 25 minutes.
   c. Using a programmable soup blender, press chunky soup.
   d. Using a manual soup blender, set cooking time for 20 minutes, then if desired blend to the consistency you require
   (Whichever is applicable to your appliance).
3. Stir in the cream & serve.

Instead of using scallops try prawns.

Scotch Broth

Ingredients **Serves 2-4**

100g Minced Lamb
25g Pearl barley
1 Carrot (peeled & sliced)
75g Swede (peeled & cubed)
1 Leek (sliced)
50g Peas (frozen)
1 Chicken stock cube
Pinch salt & pepper
1 tbsp Fresh chopped parsley

Method

1. Put the lamb, pearl barley, carrot, swede, leek, peas and stock cube in a pan or the soup maker/soup blender. If you're using a soup blender with the filter for chunky soups, place the ingredients around the outside of the filter.

2. Fill with water (approx 600ml) or to the soup level and season.
   a. Using pan method, bring to the boil and simmer for 35 minutes.
   b. Using a soup maker, use high heat setting for 7 minutes, then low/ simmer settings for 35 minutes.
   c. Using a programmable soup blender, press chunky soup.
   d. Using a manual soup blender, set cooking time for 20 minutes, then if desired blend to the consistency you require
   (Whichever is applicable to your appliance).
3. Garnish with chopped parsley and serve.

Smoked Haddock

Ingredients **Serves 2-4**

100g Smoked haddock
    (cut into 4)
1 Carrot (peeled & diced)
1 Potato (peeled & cubed)
1 Onion
    (peeled & finely chopped)
1 Chicken stock cube
1 tbsp Mascarpone
Pinch salt & pepper
1 tbsp Fresh parsley
        (chopped)
50g Sweetcorn
    (tinned or frozen)

Method

1. Put the haddock, carrot, potato, onion, stock cube, sweetcorn into a pan or the soup maker/soup blender. If you're using a soup blender with the filter for chunky soups, put the ingredients around the outside of the filter.

2. Fill with water (approx 600ml) or to the soup level and season.

    a. Using pan method, bring to the boil and simmer for 25 minutes.

    b. Using a soup maker, use high heat setting for 7 minutes, then low/simmer settings for 25 minutes.

    c. Using a programmable soup blender, press chunky soup.

    d. Using a manual soup blender, set cooking time for 20 minutes, then if desired blend to the consistency you require
    (Whichever is applicable to your appliance).

3. Stir in the mascarpone.

4. Garnish with fresh parsley and serve.

Sweet Potato & Turkey

Chunky

Ingredients **Serves 2-4**
100g Turkey mince
1 Carrot (peeled & sliced)
1 Sweet potato
  (peeled & cubed)
½ Onion
  (peeled & finely sliced)
¼ tsp Cumin
1 Chicken stock cube
2 tbsp Double cream
Pinch salt & pepper
25g Rice
1 tbsp Chopped fresh
  parsley

Method

1. Break up the turkey mince into a pan or the soup maker/soup blender then add the carrot, sweet potato, onion, cumin, rice and stock cube. If you're using a soup blender with the filter for chunky soups, place the ingredients around the outside of the filter.

2. Fill with water (approx 600ml) or to the soup level and season.
   a. Using pan method, bring to the boil and simmer for 25 minutes.
   b. Using a soup maker, use high heat setting for 7 minutes, then low/ simmer settings for 25 minutes.
   c. Using a programmable soup blender, press chunky soup.
   d. Using a manual soup blender, set cooking time for 20 minutes, then if desired blend to the consistency you require
      (Whichever is applicable to your appliance).
3. Once finished stir in the cream.
4. Garnish with fresh parsley and serve.

61

Tomato Soup with Meatballs Chunky

Ingredients **Serves 2-4**

2 Pork sausages
400g tinned chopped tomatoes
½ Onion
   (peeled & finely sliced)
1 tbsp tomato puree
1 Chicken stock cube
¼ tsp Mixed herbs
10 Fresh basil leaves
Pinch salt & pepper

Toasted french bread croutons
1 French stick (sliced)
2 tbsp Mayonnaise
45g grated Cheddar cheese

Method

1. Take the sausage out of its skin and roll into marble size meatballs.
2. Add the onion, tomatoes, tomato paste, stock cube, mixed herbs and sausage balls into a pan or the soup maker/soup blender. If you're using a soup blender with the filter for chunky soups, put the ingredients around the outside of the filter.
3. Fill with water (approx 600ml) or to the soup level and season.
   a. Using pan method, bring to the boil and simmer for 25 minutes.
   b. Using a soup maker, use high heat setting for 7 minutes, then low/ simmer settings for 25 minutes.
   c. Using a programmable soup blender, press chunky soup.
   d. Using a manual soup blender, set cooking time for 20 minutes, then if desired blend to the consistency you require
   (Whichever is applicable to your appliance).
4. To make the croutons, coat the french stick slices with mayonnaise and grated cheese, then melt under a hot grill.
5. Garnish the soup with the croutons, torn basil leaves and serve.

Try adding this to some cooked pasta, cover in cheese and bake in the oven.

Tomato & Bean with Chilli Cheese Chunky

Ingredients Serves 2-4

2 Tomatoes (quartered)
400g Tinned chopped tomatoes
400g Kidney beans in chilli
   sauce
1 Onion (peeled & quartered)
1 Red pepper
   (de-seeded & chopped)
3 tbsp Tomato sauce
½ tsp Oregano
1 Chicken stock cube
100g Chilli cheese (crumbled)
Pinch salt & pepper
10 Basil leaves

Method

1. Put the tomatoes, chopped tomatoes, onion, red pepper, tomato sauce, oregano and stock cube in a pan or the soup maker/soup blender.
2. Fill with water (approx 400ml) or to the soup level and season.
   a. Using pan method, bring to the boil and simmer for 25 minutes.
   b. Using a soup maker, use high heat setting for 7 minutes, then low/ simmer settings for 25 minutes.
   c. Using a programmable soup blender, press chunky soup.
   d. Using a manual soup blender, set cooking time for 20 minutes, then if desired blend to the consistency you require
   (Whichever is applicable to your appliance).
3. Heat the kidney beans and stir into the soup.
4. Garnish with chilli cheese torn basil leaves and serve.

Try this with tortilla chips.

65

Books Available In Our Range

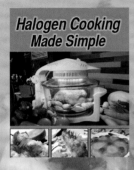

If you have any questions regarding the recipes in this book, please feel free to visit my website:

www.paulbrodel.co.uk

or email us at: **cook@paulbrodel.co.uk**